When Sam has a bath,
all his toys end up with him
in the tub, as well as the dog!

SAM'S BATH

Barbro Lindgren
illustrated by Eva Eriksson

Methuen Children's Books

First published in Great Britain 1983
by Methuen Children's Books Ltd
11 New Fetter Lane, London EC4P 4EE
First published in Sweden under the
title of *Max Balja* by Raben & Sjogren,
Stockholm, Sweden
Text copyright © 1982 Barbro Lindgren
Illustrations copyright © 1982 Eva Eriksson
This English text copyright © 1983
Methuen Children's Books Ltd

Printed in Italy
ISBN 0 416 45020 2

SAM'S BATH

Sam's going to have a bath.

He gets in the tub.
Splash!

Sam's ball goes in the tub.

Sam's truck goes in the tub.

Sam's teddy bear goes
in the tub.

Sam's biscuit goes
in the tub, too.

What about Sam's dog?
Is he going in the tub?

No! He doesn't want
to get splashed.

Sam wants his dog
to have a bath.

Splash! In goes Sam.

Splash! In goes the dog.

And they all have fun !